Basics of

Windows 7

By

Jeffrey & Nancy
Corcoran

About the Authors

Jeffrey Corcoran

A professional computer technician since 1993, Jeffrey has a wide range of experience with computer hardware and software. He has been a beta tester for *Windows 98, Windows Vista,* and *Windows 7* as well as *Office 2007* and *Internet Explorer 7* and *8*. With experience spanning from the days of DOS using computer and solving problems is old hat. Often asked for recommendations on how to learn to use computers, helping to create a book for this purpose made sense with this new Operating System.

Nancy Corcoran

Learning computers requires a healthy curiosity. This is something Nancy has always had a great deal of especially when it comes to learning new things about the computer. Mostly self taught by trying, very successfully, to figure things out on her own, she has often been called on by friends and family to guide them though their own computer difficulties.

Preface

We have found that many people have difficulties with the basic functions of Windows. This causes them much frustration and makes it much more difficult for them to learn anything further. The purpose of this book is to help people with basic functions of how to use *Windows 7*. To help with learning these basic functions, they are presented in a by the numbers method with accompanying pictures of what the screen looks like at each step. This is in no way intended to be a comprehensive instruction manual for how to use *Windows 7* nor is it intended to make you a Windows expert. What is intended is to provide how to use Windows so that you will be able to do the normal functions of using the operating system and in so doing provide a foundation for learning more advanced functions and features should you choose to do so. Even the most advanced user had to start at the beginning at some point, and without learning the basics; they never would have learned more. This book can get you up and running with how to use this new operating system for daily use, or can be your starting point as you progress into the depths of features offered. We provide the information, the path you choose is up to you.

Trademark Acknowledgments

Windows 98, Windows Vista, Windows 7, Office 2007, Internet Explorer 7, Internet Explorer 8, Windows Live, Aero, and *ReadyBoost* are registered trademarks of *Microsoft Corporation. Basics of Windows 7* is an independent publication and is not affiliated with, nor has it been authorized, sponsored, or otherwise approved by *Microsoft Corporation*.

Contents

Chapter 1 Make *Windows* Look the Way You Want........................ 1

    Adjust Screen Resolution...1

    Resize the Text to make it more readable 4

    Using Desktop Preview...6

    Personalize the appearance of *Windows*...9

        Themes 9

        Change Desktop Icons 11

        Desktop Background...13

        Windows Colors 14

        Sounds..15

        Screen Saver...16

    Automatic Window Sizing..18

    Jump list for Reopening Screens 20

    Hide the Taskbar to Get More Screen Space 21

    Control the Notification Area Icons 22

    Display a Clock for Another Time Zone 23

    Lock Your Computer to Prevent Others from Using It.........................25

    Change Shut down button 27

Chapter 2 Working with Programs 29

    Pinning to Taskbar..29

    Display preferred Programs on Your Start Menu..................................32

Unpin Programs on Your Start Menu or Taskbar 34

Uninstall a Program 36

Run a Program with Elevated Privileges 38

Create Desktop Shortcuts 40

Run a Program in Compatibility Mode 42

Chapter 3 Protecting your Computer 44

Safeguard Your Computer with a System Image Backup 44

Maintenance 48

Recycle Bin 54

System Restore 57

Chapter 4 Features of *Internet Explorer 8* 61

View Web Pages Privately 61

Protect Children by Activating Parental Controls 63

Configuring the Popup Blocker 66

Configure Tabs 68

Save Time by using Tabs 71

Add Quick launch Favorite sites 73

Remove Quick launch Favorite sites 74

Open Multiple Pages When You Start *Internet Explorer* 75

Internet Explorer 8 Search suggestions 77

Adding Search Engines 78

Remove Search Engines 80

Customize the Favorites...81

Delete Your Browsing History to Ensure Privacy..............................83

Chapter 5 Using the Control Panel 85

Allow a Program through Windows Firewall...................................85

Limit problems before they start...89

Create a Custom Power Plan to Improve Battery Life.....................94

Define Actions for Power Buttons..99

Change a Disk Drive's Letter..102

View the Current Status of Your Network.....................................106

Run the Network diagnostics Tool to Repair Problems................109

Share music and videos..113

Creating a User Account...117

Add a Password to a User Account..120

Remove or change a Password to a User Account.......................123

Deleting a User Account...127

Hear an Alert When You Press Toggle Keys.................................130

Change pointer settings including motion and visibility. 133

Change Double click speed..137

Scan for Spyware to Remove Malicious Software........................141

Configure AutoPlay Actions...145

Chapter 6 Enhancing Your *Windows* Experience........................ 148

Renaming a file...148

Change a Drive Name 151

Encrypt Confidential Files and Folders.. 153

Mapping a Network Drive 156

Share a folder with Other Users on the network 159

Find Files Faster by Sorting and Filtering 162

Restore a Previous Version of a File... 164

Protect a File by Making It Read-Only 167

Open a File with a Different Program 170

Open file or folder with single click... 173

Share drives with older computers 176

Chapter 7 Getting enjoyment from using *Windows* 180

Add the Run Command to the Start Menu... 180

Improve Performance with a USB flash Drive... 182

HomeGroup 184

Better device management... 186

Adjust Rip Settings... 188

Create an Automatic Playlist... 190

Chapter 8 Presenting with *Windows* 192

Rotate an Image 192

Snipping Tool 197

Fax and Scan 200

Magnifier 202

Speech Recognition 206

Notepad or WordPad.. 217

Windows Live Essentials... 221

Terms 223

Index... 226

Chapter 1
Make *Windows* Look the Way You Want

The way *Windows* appears can be changed to fit your particular taste and style. Some items that can be changed, such as the screen resolution or themes will have an effect on other aspects of *Windows* operation, while others like desktop background, sounds, and screen saver are for esthetics only.

Adjust Screen Resolution

The screen resolution specifies how many pixels, or dots, are used to make up the screen display. The higher the resolution the more pixels are used to make up the screen. This has two effects on what you see. First, it makes the display sharper with less blur or jaggedness. Second, it causes more space to be available on the screen as each images are smaller due to the higher density of the dots being used to make up the image so more can be displayed on the screen at one time.

1. Right click on desktop (default background)

2.   Click **Screen Resolution**

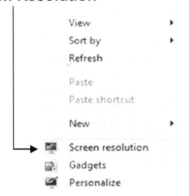

3.   Click pull down menu next to **Resolution**

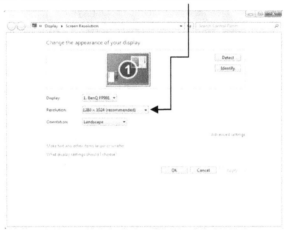

4. Move slider to desired resolution by dragging pointer
    (note: screen icon 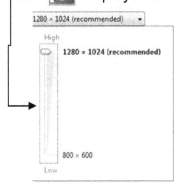 displays changes)

5. Click on open area once

6. Click **OK**

Resize the Text to make it more readable

As a side effect of higher screen resolutions, the text size is also reduced. For people with less than perfect vision this can prove to be a hindrance in using the computer. As a way to compensate for this, the text size can be changed independently of the rest of the screen settings. This allows the words to be larger than standard to make it easier to read while still taking advantage of higher screen resolutions.

1.   Right click on desktop (default background)

2.   Click **Screen Resolution**

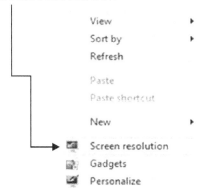

3.   Click **Make text and other items larger or smaller**

4.   Select size by moving bubble and click **Apply**

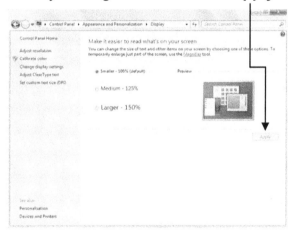

Using Desktop Preview

A great enhancement over the preview attempt that was done in *Windows Vista* is the preview of open programs. In *Windows 7,* this feature is actually useful. Any program that is open can be previewed both in a thumbnail and full screen view without having to make it the active program. This feature does require your system to have a decent video card however.

1.   Hover pointer over active program, for example *Windows Explorer*

2.   For preview to be displayed

3. Hover pointer over Preview for full size preview

4. Click preview to make it the activate window

5.   When more than one window of the same program is open, they all
display

Personalize the appearance of *Windows*

The general appearance of *Windows* can be changed from the default to fit your liking. What you see is not the only way it can be. Choose from the options for background pictures, screen savers, sounds, or put your favorite sounds and pictures on your computer and use those to give your computer a unique look.

Themes

Themes are the overall display scheme that *Windows* uses. Some theme options are restricted due to hardware performance of the computer that *Windows* is currently running. For example, people with higher performance video cards; you can take advantage of the option to have thumbnail previews of open programs by hovering your mouse pointer over that program's icon in the taskbar. Think of the theme as the general look and feel for *Windows* and then fine tune with specific options afterwards to make it just the way you like it.

1. Right click on Desktop (default background)

2.   Click **Personalize**

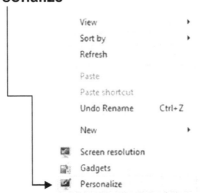

3.   Under **My Themes** would show any custom themes created. The next row is **Aero Themes**. The last row is **Basic and High Contrast Themes** for less powerful computers and for those visually impaired. Select theme by clicking on thumbnail.

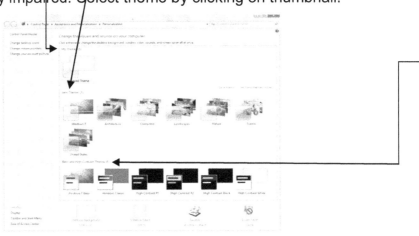

Change Desktop Icons

Adding or removing the system icons on the desktop is a very easy process now. With simply adding or removing a check from appropriate boxes, the associated icon will be added to or removed from the desktop.

1. Click **Change desktop icons** on left panel

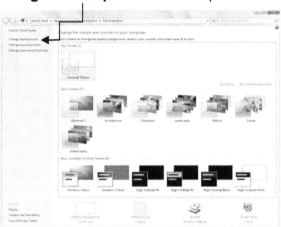

2.　　Under **Desktop icons**, select to show on desktop or unselect to hide.

3.　　Click **OK**

Desktop Background

The background picture can be changed independently from the theme so you can have any of the available pictures, or your favorite picture that you have put on your computer, displayed as your desktop background.

1.   Click **Desktop Background**

2.   After making changes, click **Save changes**

Windows Colors

The colors that each window has can be changed to fit the way you like best. By using these options, you can set the background color for desktops that do not use a picture, the text and action bar colors, and many other things. A preview is provided so you can see how things will look as you make changes without having to put everything into effect before knowing how it will work.

1.   Click **Window Color**

2.   Select color and intensity for background or click **Advance appearance settings...** for more options (NOTE: Low end video cards will skip this step)

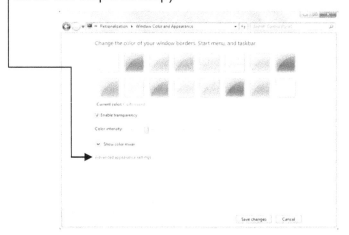

3. Using pull down menus make selection and click **OK**

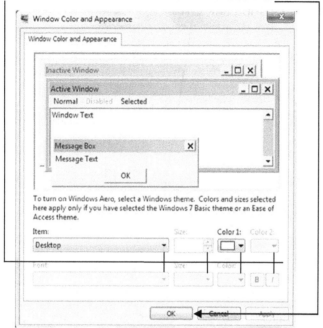

Sounds

Sounds can be set to play what you like when events occur. You can use general sound schemes to set several sound event settings at once or go through and select your own sound that you want for each event.

1. Click **Sounds**

2.   Use pull down menus or select individual event sounds to make selection and click **OK**

Screen Saver

With LCD monitors, screen savers are not as important as they once were. Having the computer go into low power mode is a more economical way of protecting the screen from the hazards of long times of non-use. Screen savers can be used for a way of adding a personal touch to your computer. Have a pattern of colors displayed, or even a slideshow of your favorite photos.

1.   Click **Screen Saver**

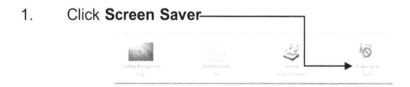

2.   Using pull down menus make selection and click **OK**

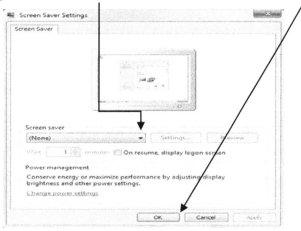

Automatic Window Sizing

A new feature in *Windows 7* is its ability to automatically resize a window to fit on your screen. This makes it extremely easy to place windows side by side for a split screen effect without having to struggle with resizing each window to try to make it fit without overlapping.

1.   Dragging to top for automatic full screen

2.   Dragging to side (example to right) for automatic half screen

Jump list for Reopening Screens

Widows 7 learns what you do and tries to make it easier to reopen these things without having to search for their prior location. Therefore, if you have been using *Windows Explorer* to view images, your jump list will include a link taking you directly to your images folder. Similarly, frequently visited web pages in *Internet Explorer* will appear on your jump list allowing you to quickly and easily reopen that page.

1. Right click on program icon on taskbar

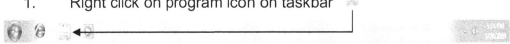

2. Most frequently used areas are automatically listed and replaced. Click what/where you want to go.

Hide the Taskbar to Get More Screen Space

Sometimes a little more desktop space can go a long way. If this is something you need, the option to have the taskbar hide is for you. When enabled the taskbar will disappear off the screen allowing for more space on your desktop, and reappear when you move your mouse pointer to the bottom of the screen.

1.   Right click on open space of Taskbar

2.   Click **Properties**

3.   Select **Auto-hide the taskbar**, then click **OK**

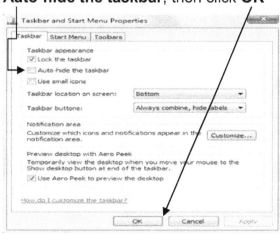

Control the Notification Area Icons

The notification area displays your currently running background programs and other features. Before you only had the option to show everything or hide what *Windows* considered inactive. This has changed with *Windows 7* and you now have the option to set each one of the notification icons individually to either display all the time, only when the program is notifying you of something, or never so that the icon is always hidden.

1.   Click icon ▲ for "show hidden icons"

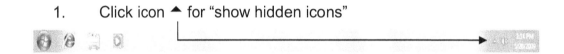

2.   Click **Customize...**

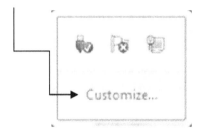

3.   Using pull down menus make selection and click **OK**

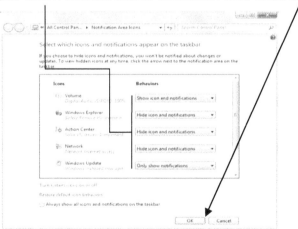

Display a Clock for Another Time Zone

You may work with someone in another time zone, have a friend in one, or for whatever reason have a need to know the time in a time zone other than the one you are in. You now have the option to display more than one clock so you can easily see the time in both your current time zone and up to two additional time zones that you select.

1. Right click on clock on taskbar

2. Click **Adjust date/time**

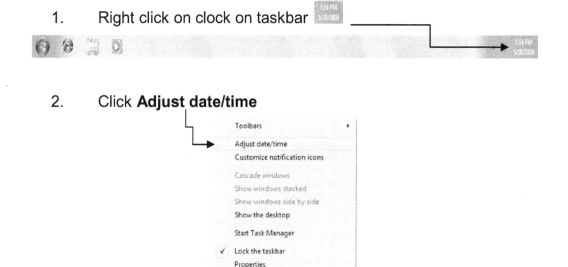

3. Click **Additional Clocks** tab (there can be a total of 3 clocks)

Select **Show this clock**

Select **Select time zone** using pull down menu

Enter **Display name**

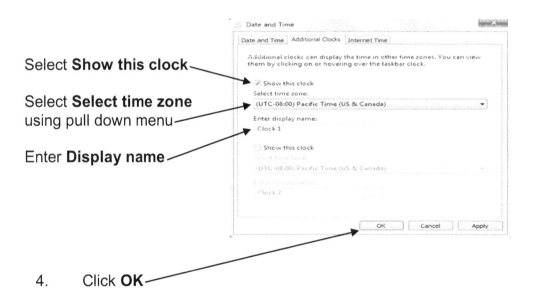

4. Click **OK**

Lock Your Computer to Prevent Others from Using It

Sometimes you need to be away from your computer, but you do not want other people messing around with it and do not want to log off the computer. For these times, you can lock your computer so your password has to be entered for your username without having to close any of your programs as would occur with logging off the system. This gives you the protection of keeping others off your computer without interfering with taking additional time and trouble for using your own computer.

1.   Click **Start**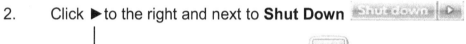

2.   Click ▶ to the right and next to **Shut Down**

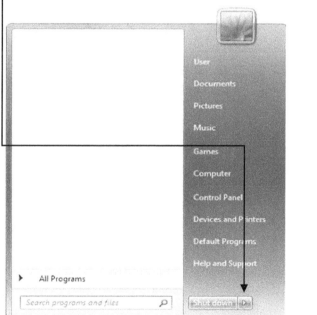

3.　　Click **Lock**

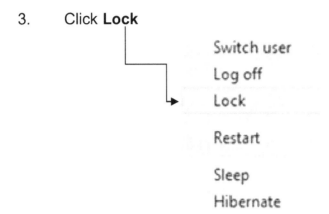

Change Shut down button

Widows 7 button defaults to the shut down function, turning off your computer. This however might not be the most common function that you use. This button can be changed to the function you do use most often.

1. Click **Start**

2. Right click on **Shut Down**

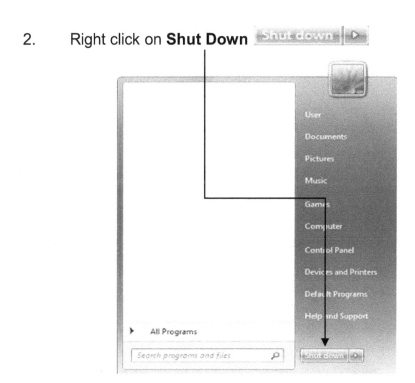

3. Click **Properties**   Properties

4. Click ▾ for pull down menu next to **Shut Down** to the right of **Power button action**

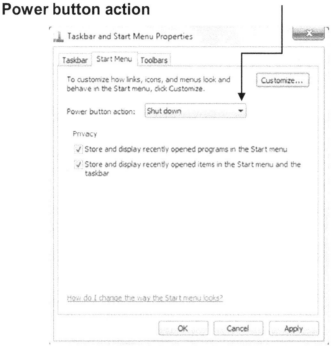

5. From pull down menu, select action to perform when power button clicked.

6. Click **OK**

7. Example: If Restart was selected

Chapter 2
Working with Programs

After you have your software home from the store and installed, you need to be able to start it in order to use it. All programs you get can be started through All Programs, but for those you use the most often you can create shortcuts to be able to start them more easily.

Pinning to Taskbars at bottom for easy access to a program with single click

Windows used to have a Quick Launch Bar on the Taskbar to let you start programs you select easily and quickly. *Windows 7* expands this giving the option to pin programs to the Taskbar creating a seamless connection between the programs being used and those ready for you to start with a single click.

1.   Click **Start**

2. Click **All Programs**

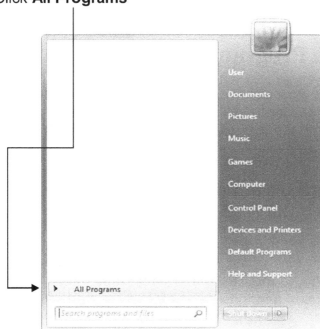

3. Right click on program to pin to taskbar (**XPS Viewer** used to demonstrate)

4. Click **Pin to Taskbar**

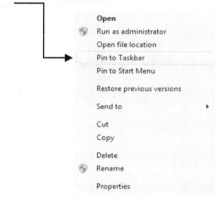

Taskbar before pinning

Taskbar after pinning

Basics of *Windows 7*

Page | **32**

Display preferred Programs on Your Start Menu

The new Start menu gives a large section where recently used programs automatically appear. This can also be a handy place for frequently used programs so they remain without changing, but you do not want to have them on the Taskbar.

1.　　Click **Start**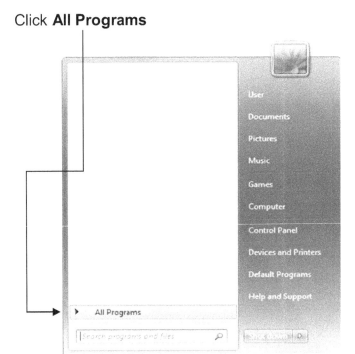

2.　　Click **All Programs**

3.　　Right click program to keep on Start Menu

4. Click **Pin to Start Menu**

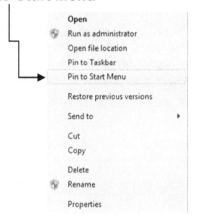

Unpin Programs on Your Start Menu or Taskbar

Over time, you may decide that a program you once wanted to keep always available is not high on your list any longer. If this happens, you can unpin this program from your Start Manu or Taskbar, freeing up this space for something you do use more often.

To unpin from Start Menu

1. Click **Start**

2. Right click on program to unpin

3.　　Click **Unpin from Start Menu**

To unpin from Taskbar

1.　　Right click on program to unpin

2.　　Click **Unpin this program from taskbar**

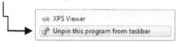

Uninstall a Program

Over time, you will want to remove programs that you no longer need or you do not need at the time so the drive space can be used for other things. This process of removing a program from your computer is called Uninstalling.

1. Click **Start**

2. Click **Control Panel**

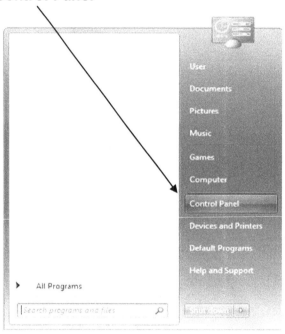

3.   Click **Uninstall a program**

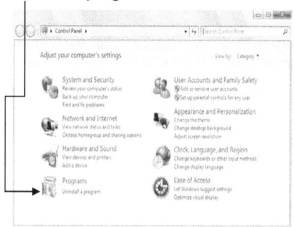

4.   Click program to uninstall then desired action

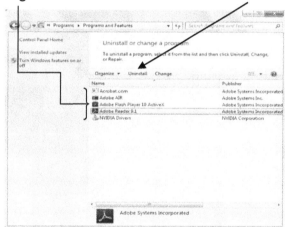

Run a Program with Elevated Privileges

If you have an account with lower level access, such as for children, some programs may require you to run that particular program with higher level of privileges than is standard with the user account. In this case, you can still use a standard account with programs that require greater privileges.

1. Click **Start**

2. Click **All Programs**

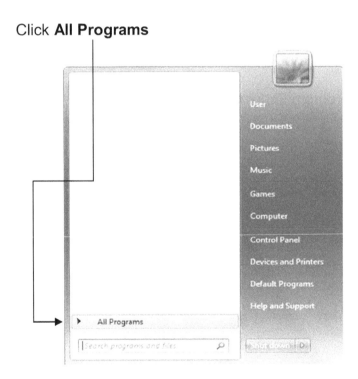

3. Right click program to elevate privileges

4.   Click **Properties**

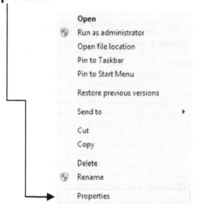

5.   Click **Compatibility** tab

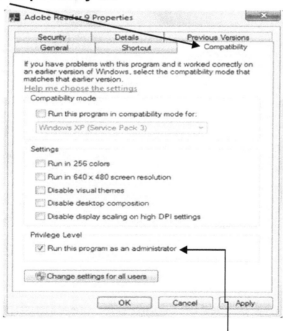

6.   Under Privilege Level, mark **Run this program as an administrator**

7.   Click **OK**

Create Desktop Shortcuts

For some, the easiest way to access a program is to double click on a desktop icon. This is not an efficient way to organize programs but on particular programs, it can be more convenient

1. Click **Start**

2. Click **All Programs**

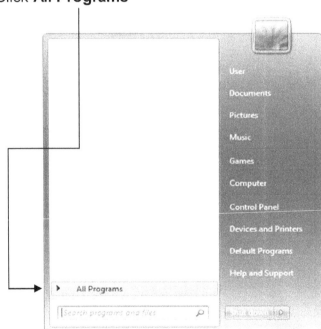

3. Put mouse pointer on program for creating shortcut

4. Hold right mouse button down and drag mouse pointer to desktop

5.   Release button

6.   Click "Create shortcuts here"

Run a Program in Compatibility Mode

Having a new version of *Windows* can create difficulties when your software was written for an older version. Sometimes the old software does not want to work on the newer Operating System. *Windows* helps you around this problem by letting programs run in Compatibility Mode. This sets *Windows* to tell the program you using the older version of *Windows* that the software is designed for.

1.   Click **Start**

2.   Click **All Programs**

3.   Right click on desired program

4. Click **Properties**

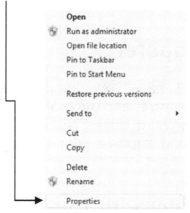

5. Click **Compatibility** tab

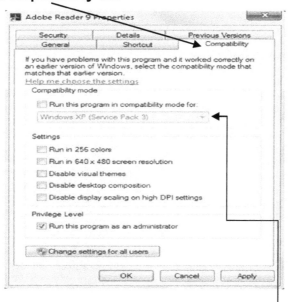

6. Under Compatibility mode, select **Run this program in compatibility mode for:** then choose operating system using pull down menu

7. Click **OK**

Chapter 3
Protecting your Computer

Regardless of how well made your computer is, things can go wrong. Between hardware failures, Malware, and general software glitches you stand to risk losing everything on your hard drive. There are things that you can do however to reduce the risk and improve your ability to recover if something catastrophic should happen.

Safeguard Your Computer with a System Image Backup

If the worst should occur and everything on your drive is lost, a system image will allow the most promising way possible to recover your data.

1.   Click **Start**

2.   Click **All Programs**

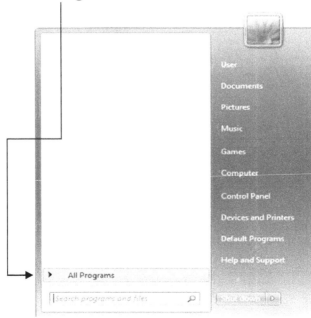

3.   Click **Maintenance**

4.   Click **Backup and Restore**

5.   On the left panel, click **Create a system image**

6.   Follow screen instructions, and then click **Next**

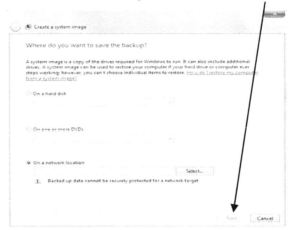

7.   Click the **Start backup**

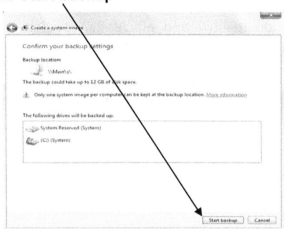

Maintenance

In order to function reliably and efficiently, regular maintenance must be performed. Updates for *Windows* are released to fix bugs, the hard drive data also becomes fragmented over time making the system run slower and adding wear to the hard drive. Both of these require maintenance. Fortunately, *Windows 7* allows for both of these functions to be done automatically once it is set up.

Windows Update

1. Click **Start**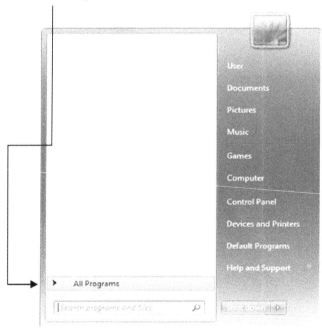

2. Click **All Programs**

3. Click **Windows Update**

4. On left panel, click **Change settings**

5.   Select options for getting updates and then click **OK**

NOTE: If automatic is not selected, updates will need to be gotten manually by clicking **Install updates**

Disk Defragmenter

1.   Click Start

2.   Click **All Programs**

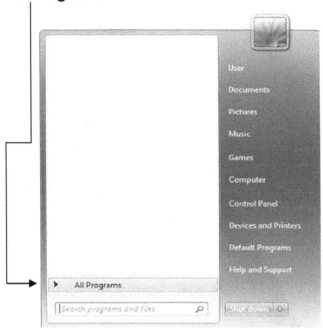

3.   Click **Accessories**

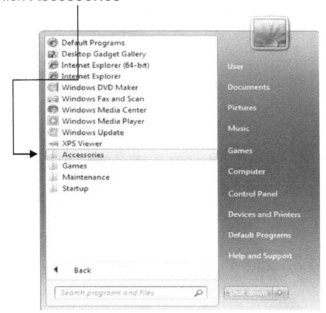

4.   Click **System Tools**

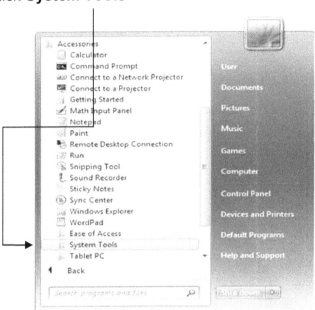

5.   Click **Disk Defragmenter**

6.   Click **Configure schedule…**

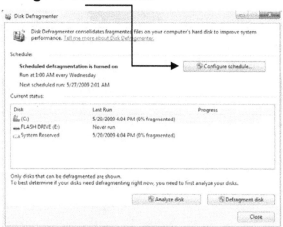

7.   Use pull down menus to configure schedule and then click **OK**

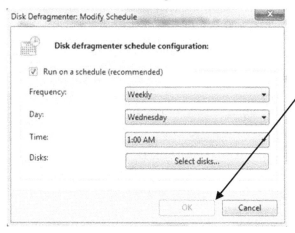

Recycle Bin

When files are first deleted, they are not actually gone. Deleted files are moved to the recycle bin. This is a midpoint before being truly deleted. Files that are in the recycle bin can be restored, so anything you deleted by mistake can be recovered without difficulty. After files are emptied from the recycle bin, they are then truly deleted.

To Restore

1.   Double click Recycle Bin

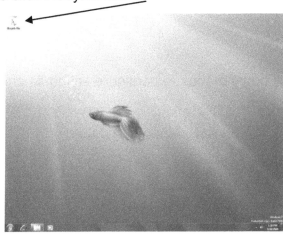

(default desktop)

2. Click **Restore all items** for everything in bin, or click each item. The **Restore all items** will change to **Restore this item**

To Empty

1. Right click Recycle Bin

2. Click **Empty Recycle Bin**

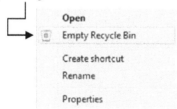

3. If multiple items, click **Yes** on this screen

4.   If single item, click **Yes** on this screen.

Once items are deleted from Recycle Bin they cannot be restored

System Restore

Windows is able to help you recover from serious problems automatically. During installations and other times, *Windows* will create Restore Points, which can be used to take your computer back to a previous time. When things go very wrong, using System Restore will often correct the problem and make things as if the problem never happened.

1.   Click **Start**

2.   Click **All Programs**

3.   Click **Accessories**

4.   Click **System Tools**

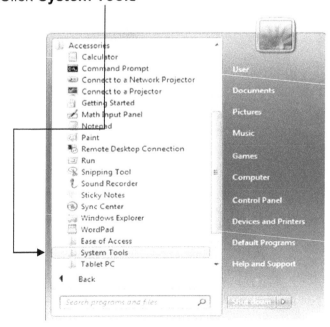

5. Click **System Restore**

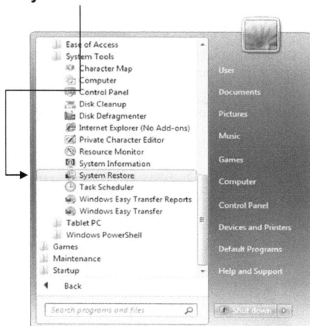

6. Click **Next**

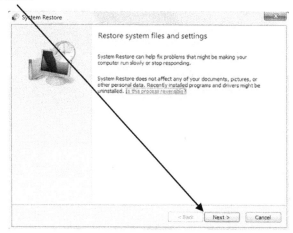

7.   If there is only one recommended restore point, just click **Next**.

8.   If there is more than one restore point, this screen will show a selection for which point to use.

9.   Click **Finish**

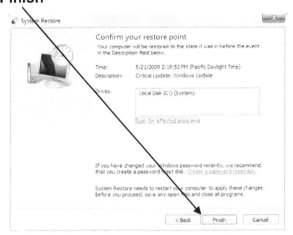

Chapter 4
Features of *Internet Explorer 8*

Internet Explorer 8 has many new features and enhancements to give added privacy, protection, and convenience when browsing the web and handling favorites. This not only makes it less frustrating to view web sites but also helps to keep your information protected from snoops and gives added protection when your children view websites.

View Web Pages Privately

There are times you might not want what you are viewing on the web to be visible to others, such as planning a surprise gift for example. For these times, InPrivate Browsing lets you view web sites as usual but leave no tracks behind on what sites you were looking at.

1.   Click *Internet Explorer* icon on Taskbar

2.   Click **Safety** on command bar at top right

3.   Click **InPrivate Browsing**

4.   Use as usual

Protect Children by Activating Parental Controls

There are some sites you just do not want your kids to see. By using Parental Controls, you can establish limits on what pages your kids can view, whether they are trying to go to that site intentionally, because of error or redirecting.

1. Click *Internet Explorer* icon on Taskbar

2. Click **Tools** on command bar at top right

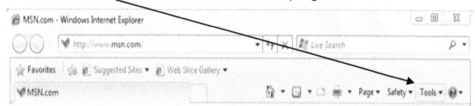

3. Click **Internet Options**

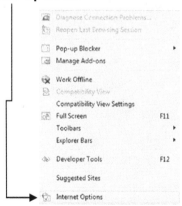

4.   Click **Content** tab, then **Parental Controls**

5.   Click which **User** Account to apply parental control

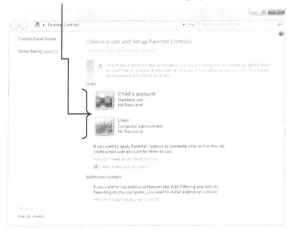

6.   Set control limits as desired

7.   Click **OK**

Configuring the Popup Blocker

Pop-ups can be both useful and an annoyance, often they are used for ads or to force you to websites that often contain malicious software. Others however are functions of websites that you want to visit. By configuring the pop-up blocker you can make *Internet Explorer* block most of the pop-ups that you do not want while allowing those you do want to come though.

1.   Click *Internet Explorer* icon on Taskbar

2.   Click **Tools** on command bar at top right

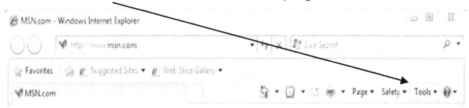

3.   Click **Internet Options**

4.   Click **Privacy** tab

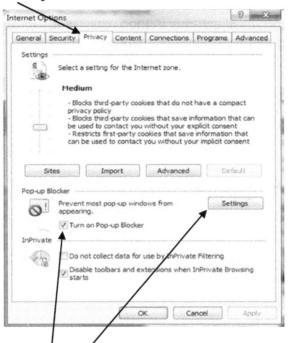

5.   **Turn on Pop-up Blocker** to prevent pop-ups

6.   Click **Settings** for additional options

Configure Tabs

Tabs allow you to view more than one website within the same web browser. Configuring this function, you can adjust this feature to suit your needs and give you the best browsing experience.

1. Click *Internet Explorer* icon on Taskbar

2. Click **Tools** on command bar at top right

3. Click **Internet Options**

4.   Click **Settings**

5.   Select Preferences

6.   Click **OK**

Save Time by using Tabs

After tabs have been configured to work the way you want them, it is time to use them. Tabs are a great convenience and can greatly enhance web browsing.

1.   Click *Internet Explorer* icon on Taskbar

2.   Click on New Tab icon

3.   Go to site for new tab

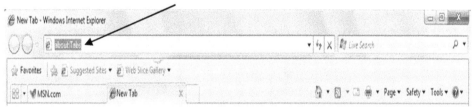

4.   View all open tabs with Quick Tabs

5. Click thumbnail to go to that tab

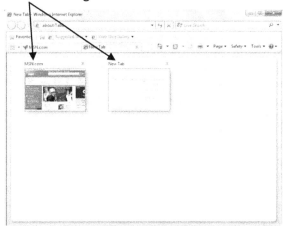

Add Quick launch Favorite sites

A new feature in *Internet Explorer 8* is the Favorites Bar. This is a quick launch for favorite sites that you can go to with a single click. This is not a replacement for the normal Favorites menu but a companion to it to make certain sites easier to access.

1.   Click *Internet Explorer* icon on Taskbar

2.   Go to desired website

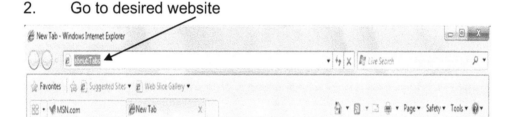

3.   Click **Add to Favorites Bar** icon

4.   New Quick Launch is added

Remove Quick launch Favorite sites

If a site is no longer wanted on the Favorites Bar, it can be removed, giving more space for new ones to be added or to simply get them out of the way.

1.   Right click Quick launch favorite to remove, then click **Delete**

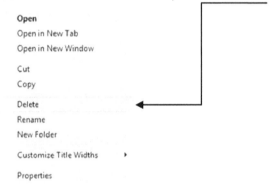

2.   Click **Yes**

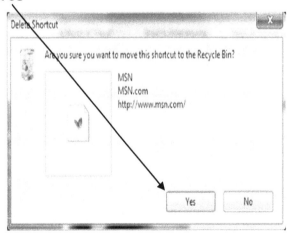

Open Multiple Pages When You Start *Internet Explorer*

When *Internet Explorer* starts, it can automatically bring up a web page called the Home Page. You can have more than one Home Page and have them all open every time you start *Internet Explorer*.

1. Click *Internet Explorer* icon on Taskbar

2. Click **Tools** on command bar at top right

3. Click **Internet Options**

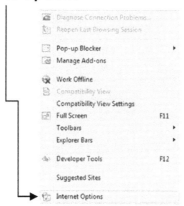

4.   Enter addresses of sites to open when *Internet Explorer* starts

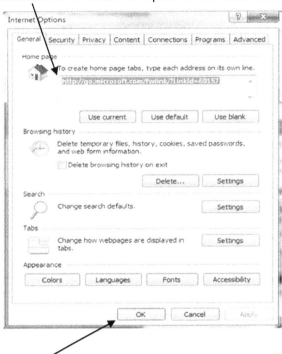

5.   Click **OK**

Internet Explorer 8 Search suggestions

As characters are typed in the search request, a list of relevant suggestions from the chosen provider are listed complete with images, if available. Search also uses your browsing history to narrow the suggestions. If what you want is listed, just click on the name.

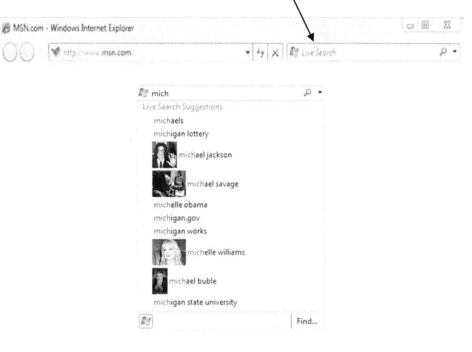

Adding Search Engines

Search Engines are used to find sites and information that you are looking for on the web. Despite what you often hear on TV, there are many search engines. To the right of the address bar in the search function where you enter what you are looking for, and can select which of the engines to use. To be able to use these engines they must first be added to your list of engines.

1. Click *Internet Explorer* icon on Taskbar

2. Click ▼ next to magnifying glass on far right

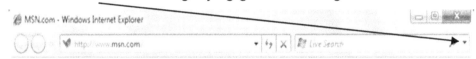

3. Click **Find More Providers...**

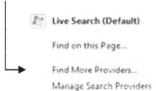

4. Click on **Add to *Internet Explorer*** for each search engine wanted. (NOTE: there are multiple pages)

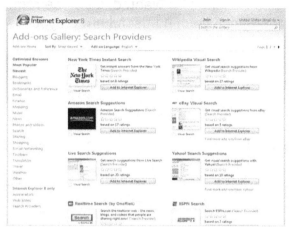

5. Click **Add**

Remove Search Engines

If a search engine no longer is wanted, it can be removed from your list so that only those search engines you find useful are on your list.

1. Click *Internet Explorer* icon on Taskbar

2. Click ▼ next to magnifying glass on far right

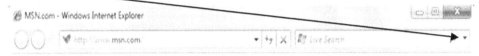

3. Click **Manage Search Providers**

4. Click on provider to remove, then click **Remove**

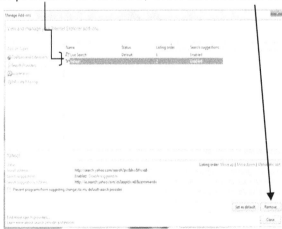

Customize the Favorites

As you add web pages to your favorites, it can become very disorderly and hard to find what you are looking for. In order to get them organized so you can find what you are looking for you can customize your favorites.

1.　　Click *Internet Explorer* icon on Taskbar

2.　　Click **Favorites**

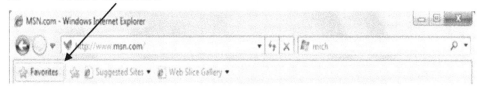

3.　　Click ▼ next to **Add to Favorites...**

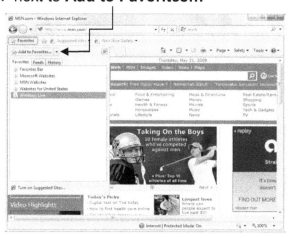

4.   Click **Organize Favorites…**

5.   Organize Favorites to your choices by using shown options

Delete Your Browsing History to Ensure Privacy

Privacy can be an important thing, and some people do not like the idea of a trail being left on what they have been viewing on the web. This can be easily removed to keep your web activity more private.

1.   Click *Internet Explorer* icon on Taskbar

2.   Click **Safety** on command bar at top right

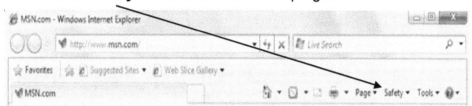

3.   Click **Delete Browsing History...**

4.   Check everything to delete, then click **Delete** at bottom

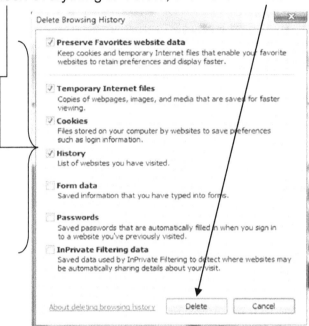

Chapter 5
Using the Control Panel

The central control area for adjusting how *Windows* works can be found under the Control Panel. There is a massive amount of options and while this book cannot possibility cover all of them, many key functions and features are covered here to allow you to get *Windows* configured and running smoothly.

Allow a Program through *Windows* Firewall

The firewall is designed to keep unwanted programs from sending data through the Internet. Sometimes you want programs to be able to send information though in order to do its job. To allow this you can set an exception so the firewall will allow only those programs you specify to pass data through while still blocking all others.

1.   Click **Start**

2.   Click **Control Panel**

3.   Click **System and Security**

4.   Click **Allow a program through Windows Firewall** under the
      Windows Firewall heading

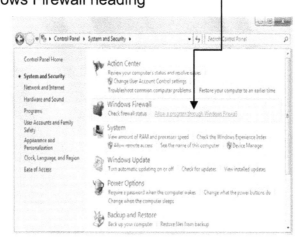

5.   Click **Change settings**

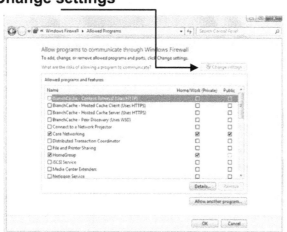

6.   Choose from selections if listed, else click **Allow another program...**

7.   Select program to include then click **Add**

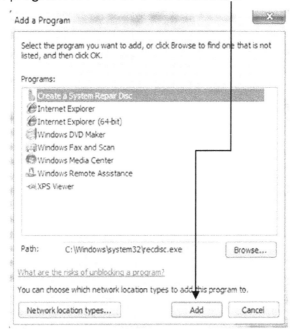

8.   Click **OK** when finished

Limit problems before they start

Windows has built in features to prevent malicious software from causing problems. You can receive alerts when programs try to run and warnings when other safeguards are not in place so you can take preventive action.

1.   Click **Start**

2.   Click **Control Panel**

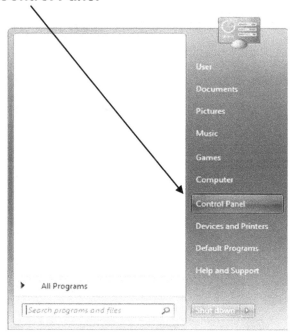

3. Click **System and Security**

4. Click **Action Center**

5. Click **Change Action Center settings** on the left panel

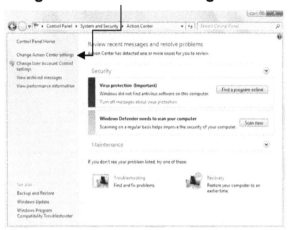

6. Select warnings wanted, then click **OK**

7. Click **Change User Account Control settings** on the left panel

8. Drag slider for the desired amount of notice then click **OK**

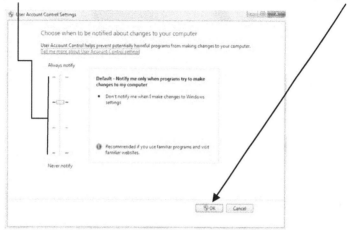

Create a Custom Power Plan to Improve Battery Life

Battery life is a very important aspect of mobile computing. A simple way to get the most run time from your battery is by adjusting your power plan. This sets your computer not to waste power on things that are not a priority, such as reducing processor power in exchange for longer usable time.

1.   Click **Start**

2.   Click **Control Panel**

3.   Click **System and Security**

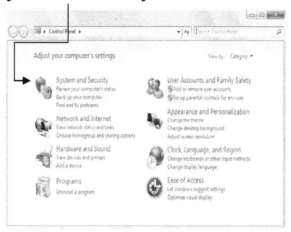

4.   Click **Power Options**

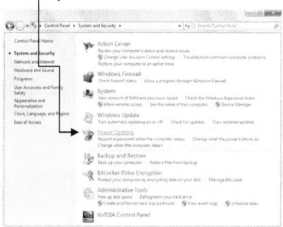

5.   To create a customized setting, click **Create a power plan** on the left panel

6.   Follow instructions on screen, then click **Next**

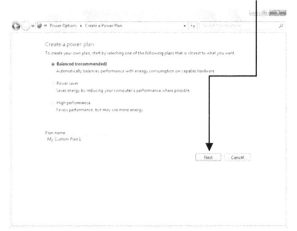

7.   Select preferences using the pull down menus, then click **Create**

8.   Click **Change plan settings** next to the plan just made to customize

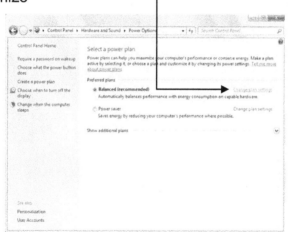

9. Make basic changes on this screen or click **Change advanced power settings**

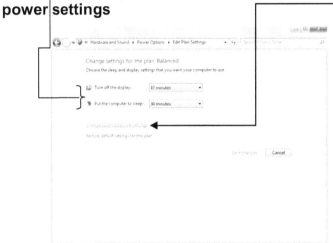

10. Follow instructions on screen (scroll for more options)

11. Click **OK**

Define Actions for Power Button

You can change the action that *Windows* takes when you press your computer's power button. This can be set to shut off the computer, place it into hibernate, standby mode, or even to do nothing. When using a notebook you can also specify the action that *Windows* takes when you close the lid in a similar fashion.

1. Click **Start**

2. Click **Control Panel**

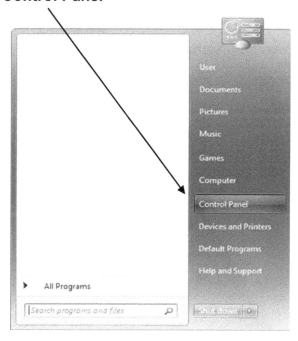

3. Click **System and Security**

4. Click **Power Options**

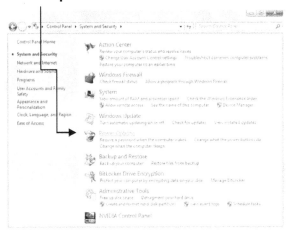

5. Click **Choose what the power button does** on the left panel

6. Select preferences using the pull down menus, then click **Save changes**

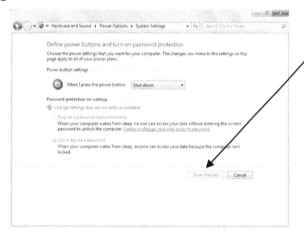

Change a Disk Drive's Letter

The default drive letter is not always the letter that you want assigned to a particular drive. If this should be the case, you can change the drive letter assignment so it does fit your needs.

1.   Click **Start**

2.   Click **Control Panel**

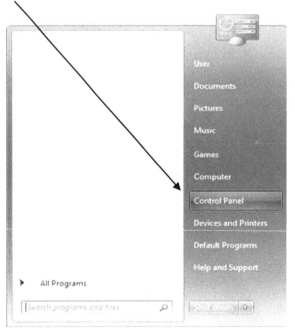

3. Click on **System and Security**

4. Click **Administrative Tools**

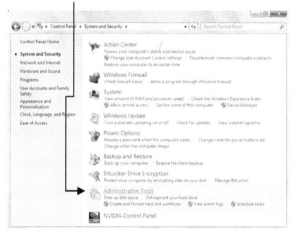

5.   Double click **Computer Management**

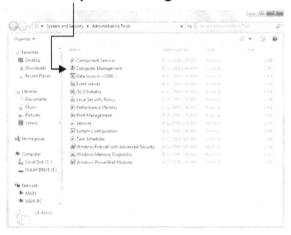

6.   Click **Disk Management**

7.   Right click on the drive the letter is to be changed

8.　　Click **Change Drive Letter and Paths...**

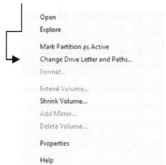

9.　　Take the appropriate actions

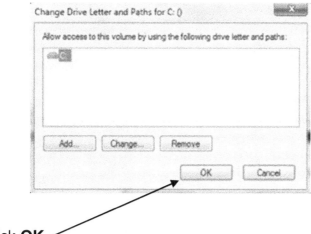

10.　Click **OK**

View the Current Status of Your Network

Checking the status of your network lets you quickly determine how your network is configured and spot any problems that may be occurring.

1.   Click **Start**

2.   Click **Control Panel**

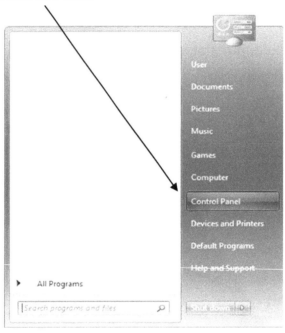

3.   Click **Network and Internet**

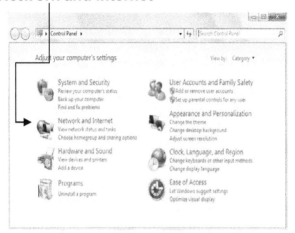

4.   Click **Network and Sharing Center**

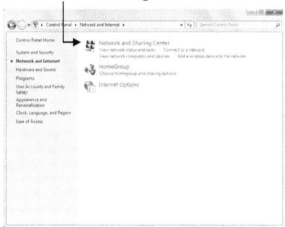

5.   When viewing is complete, close window by clicking **red X** square in upper right corner

Run the Network diagnostics Tool to Repair Problems

If there is a problem with your network and you cannot seem to find why, the network diagnostic tool runs automated tests to determine the problem and in many cases repair the issue to get your network running properly.

1.   Click **Start**

2.   Click **Control Panel**

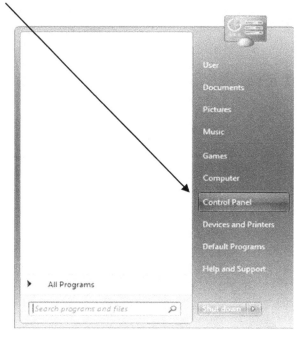

3.   Click **Network and Internet**

4.   Click **Network and Sharing Center**

5.　　Click **Troubleshoot problems**

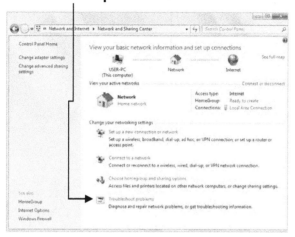

6.　　Click area to diagnose problem

7.   Click **Next**

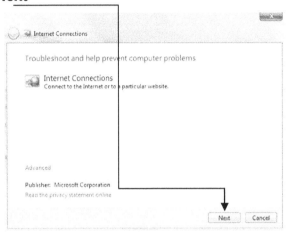

8.   When completed, click **Close the troubleshooter**

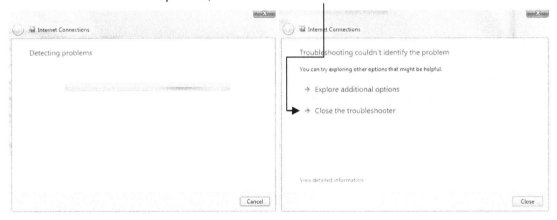

Share music and videos

Your digital media, such as music and video files, can be set for sharing between other computers on your network. This can be easier than copying your files to each computer you want to play them.

1.   Click **Start**

2.   Click **Control Panel**

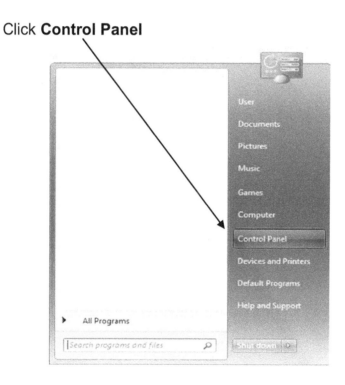

3.   Click **Network and Internet**

4.   Click **Network and Sharing Center**

5.   Click **Change advanced sharing settings** on the left panel

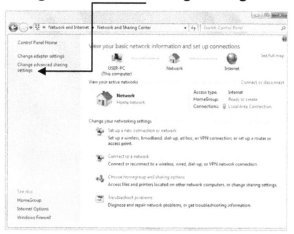

6.   Under **Media streaming** click **Choose media streaming options…**

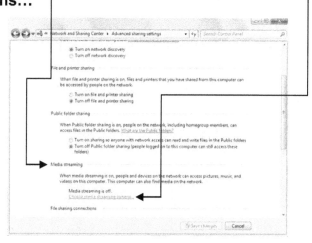

7.   By default, media streaming is OFF

8.   To turn on, click **Turn on media streaming**

9.   Choose **Allowed** or **Blocked** from pull down menu for sharing preference then **OK**

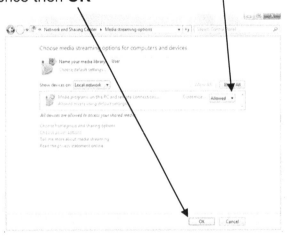

Creating a User Account

Windows lets you have more than one user account so you can restrict access for other users, such as children, who you do not want to have full access to everything. "Administrators" have unrestricted access to everything while "standard" users have limited access. Note: some software must be run as an administrator in order to function.

1.   Click **Start**

2.   Click **Control Panel**

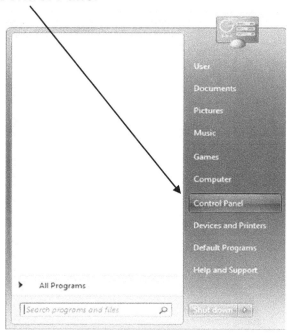

3.   Click **Add or Remove User Account**

4.   Click **Create a new account**

5.   Enter **New account name**, select account type, click **Create Account**

Add a Password to a User Account

People can make a mess out of things if they get into your system or account without permission. This can be anything from seeing private files you do not want seen, to damaging or deleting your data. To prevent this from happening you can set a password that has to be entered before accessing your user account. This will help ensure that the only ones that access your data are yourself or those you give permission.

1.　　Click **Start**

2.　　Click **Control Panel**

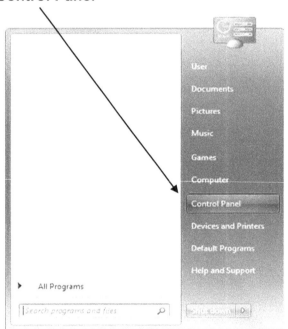

3.   Click **Add or remove user accounts**

4.   Click account for password

5.   Click **Create a password**

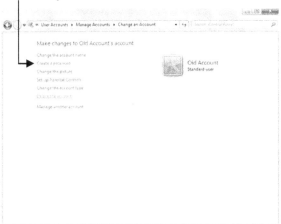

6.   Enter **New password** and **Type a password hint** (optional)

7.   Click **Create password**

Remove or change a Password to a User Account

At some point you might decide a different password would be better to have, either your taste changes or for security. You may even decide you no longer need a password at all. In either case, it is very easy to change or remove the password associated with any user account.

1. Click **Start**

2. Click **Control Panel**

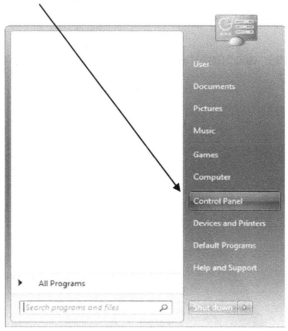

3. Click **Add or remove user accounts**

4. Click user account that will get the password change or password deleted

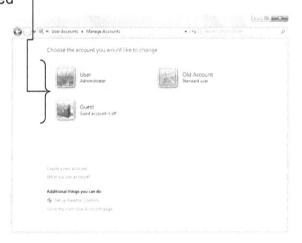

5.   Click either **Change the password** or **Remove the password**

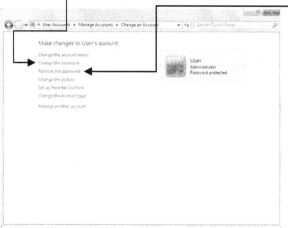

To change password

Enter appropriate information, then click **Change password**

To delete password from standard account

Click **Remove Password**

To delete password from administrator account

Enter **Current password**, then click **Remove Password**

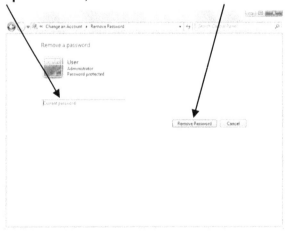

Deleting a User Account

As with everything, needs change. A user account you made before may no longer be of any use. User accounts that are no longer needed can be deleted.

1.   Click **Start**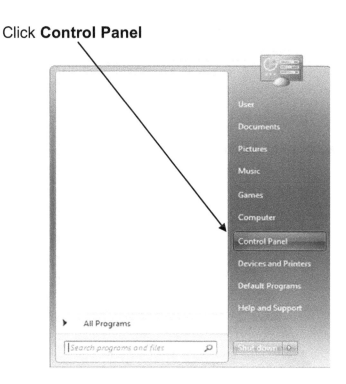

2.   Click **Control Panel**

3. Click **Add or Remove User Accounts**

4. Click account to delete

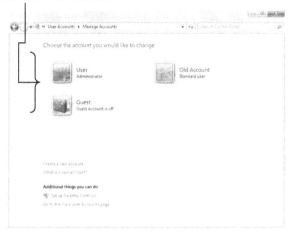

5.   Click **Delete the account**

6.   Click your choice of **Delete Files** or **Keep Files** associated with this account

7.   Click **Delete Account** to confirm

Hear an Alert When You Press the CAPS LOCK, NUM LOCK, or SCROLL LOCK (Toggle Keys).

These alerts can help prevent the frustration of inadvertently pressing a key and not realizing it.

1. Click **Start**

2. Click **Control Panel**

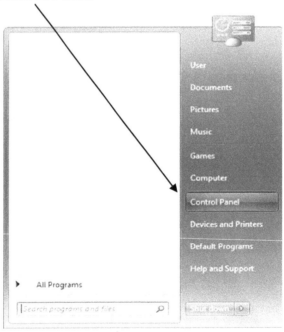

3.　　Click **Ease of Access**

4.　　Click **Ease of Access Center**

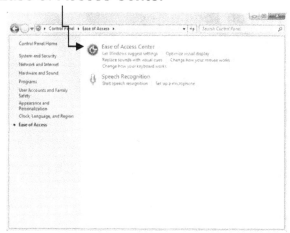

5. Under **Explore all settings**, select **Make the keyboard easier to use**

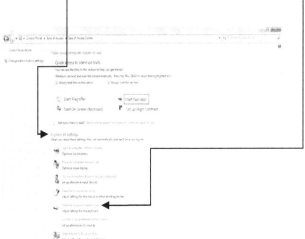

6. Select **Turn on Toggle Keys**

7. Click **OK**

Change mouse pointer behavior settings

The way the mouse pointer responds to your input can be adjusted so that is it easier for you to use your mouse and makes using your computer less frustrating.

1.   Click **Start**

2.   Click **Control Panel**

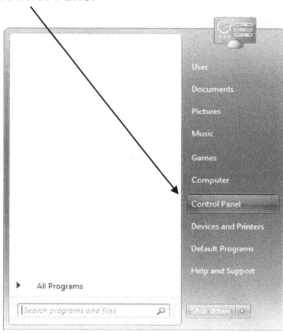

3.　　Click **Ease of Access**

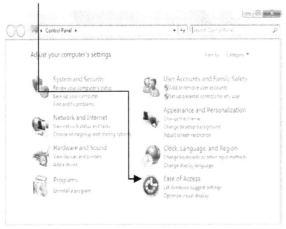

4.　　Click **Ease of Access Center**

5.   Under **Explore all Settings**, select **Make the mouse easier to use**

6.   Click **Mouse settings**

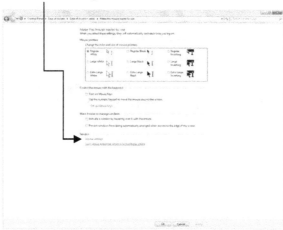

7.   In **Mouse Properties,** select the **Pointer Options** tab

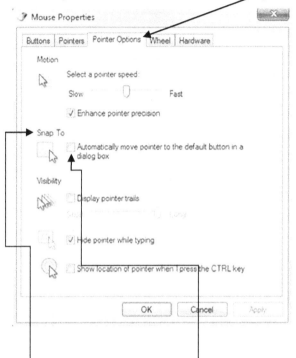

8.   Under **Snap To**, select **Automatically move pointer to the default button in a dialog box** then click **OK**

Change Double click speed

Not everyone's hands work the same. For some people, the default speed for double clicking the mouse button may be very difficult to do. The speed at which the mouse button must be clicked for the double click function can be adjusted to make it easier for your particular use.

1. Click **Start**

2. Click **Control Panel**

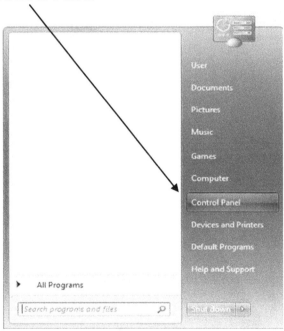

3. Click **Ease of Access**

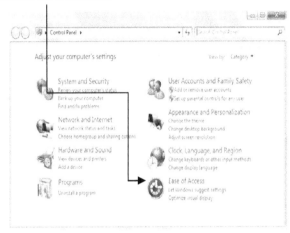

4. Click **Ease of Access Center**

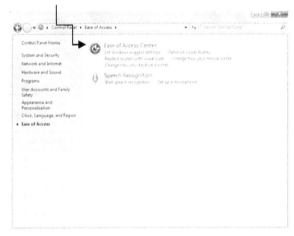

5.   Under **Explore all settings**, select **Make the mouse easier to use**

6.   Click **Mouse Settings**

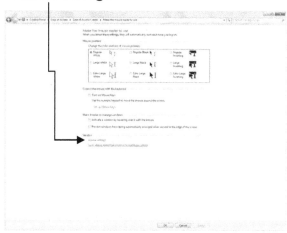

7. Drag slider for double click speed then double click for testing.

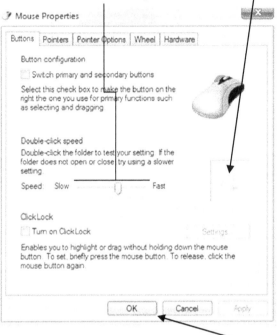

8. Repeat until desired speed is obtained then click **OK**

Scan for Spyware to Remove Malicious Software

Windows has built in protection against spyware and other malicious software called **Windows Defender**.

1. Click **Start**

2. Click **Control Panel**

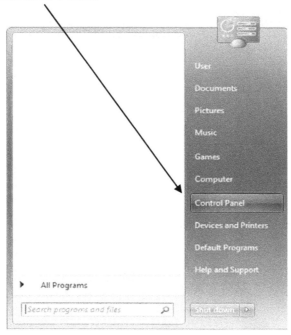

3.   Click **Category** to right of View by: for pull down menu

4.   Click either of the icon options

⊙ Category

Large icons

Small icons

5.   Click **Windows Defender**

6.   Click **Scan** to scan hard drive

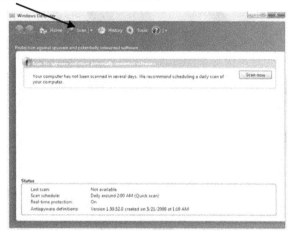

or to change options

7.   Click **Tools**

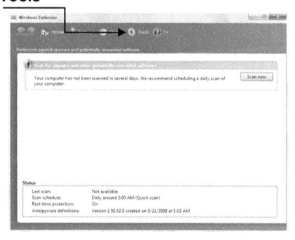

8.   Click **Options**

9.   Click which options to configure then click **Save**

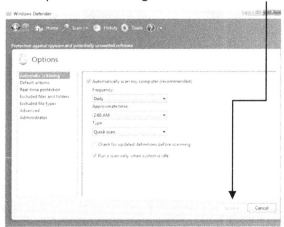

Configure AutoPlay Actions

AutoPlay is the automatically running of a program with removable media in put in the drive. This can be the setup program for a new piece of software for making install easy, or the music or video player when an audio CD or movie DVD is placed in the drive.

1. Click **Start**

2. Click **Control Panel**

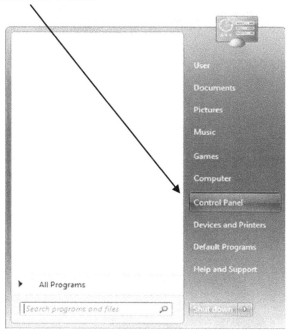

3.   Click **Category** to right of View by: for pull down menu

4.   Click either of the icon options

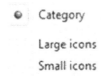

5.   Click **AutoPlay**

6. Under **Choose what happens when you insert each type of media or device**, select **Use AutoPlay for all media and devices**, or select items individually.

7. Click **Save**

Chapter 6
Enhancing Your *Windows* Experience

Windows has many features and options to allow you to get the most enjoyment from your computer. These can be as simple as a new name to something more advanced like the way you click a file to open it.

Renaming a file

You may not always like the name a file came with, or that you gave it when creating the file. In these instances, you can rename the file to something more suitable or that you like better.

1.   Click **Start**

2.   Click **Computer**

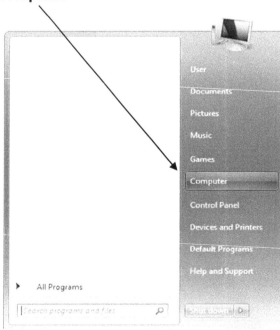

3.   Click **Documents** under **Libraries** or document location

4.   Right click on filename to change

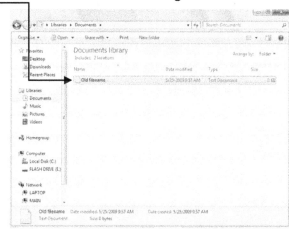

5.   Click **Rename**

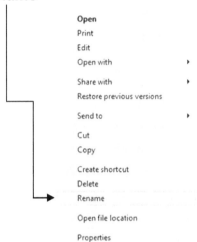

6.   Enter new filename and press the **ENTER** key

Change a Drive Name

Just as files can be renamed, so can drives. This can make it easier or organize your data so that a drive will have an actual, useful name rather than "removable drive" or "local drive" as with the default names.

1.   Click **Start**

2.   Click **Computer**

3.   Right click on drive to name

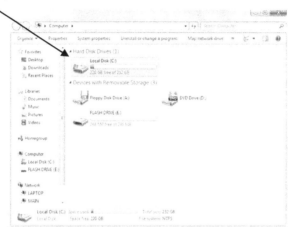

4.   Click **Rename**

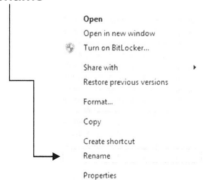

5.   Enter name for drive and press **ENTER.** Press **Continue** if this
screen displays

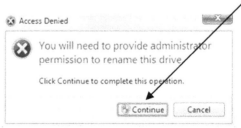

Encrypt Confidential Files and Folders

For some, privacy and security are very important factors. By using encryption, you can keep these items protected from prying eyes.

1. Click **Start**

2. Click **Computer**

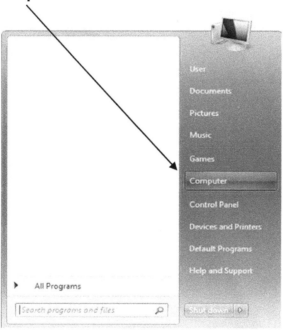

3.   Click location of file or folder to encrypt.

4.   Right click on item to encrypt and then click **Properties**

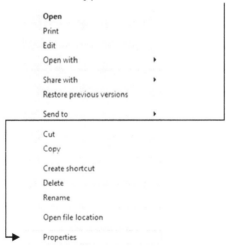

5.   Click **Advanced...**

6.   Select **Encrypt contents to secure data**

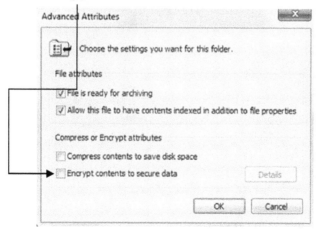

7.   Click **OK** on all windows

Mapping a Network Drive

Networked drives can be very useful for accessing data on other computers in your network, but having to located the drive each time can be bothersome. This inconvenience can be eliminated by mapping the networked drive to a local drive letter, allowing the drive to be found and accessed as easily as any drive on the computer you are working on.

1.   Click **Start**

2.   Click **Computer**

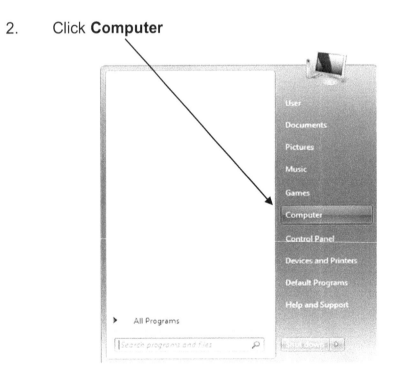

3.   Click ► next to computer with drive to map

4.   Right click drive to map

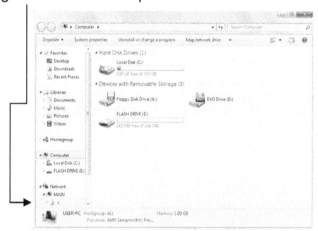

5.   Click **Map network drive...**

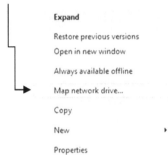

6.   Select Drive letter from pull down menu

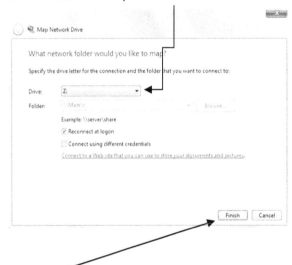

7.   Click **Finish**

Share a folder with Other Users on the network

We have seen how network drives can make sharing data easier, but to be able to use this feature the drive must first be shared. To set your drive to be shcared will allow it to be a network drive on other computers in your network.

1.   Click **Start**

2.   Click **Computer**

3. Click ▶ next to drive holding the folder to share

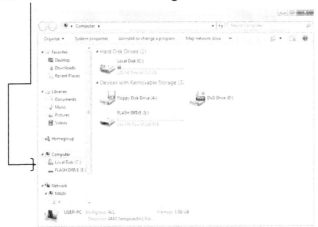

4. Right click on folder to share

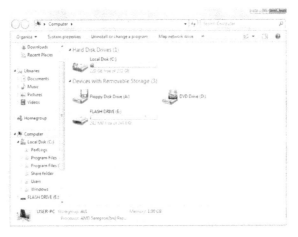

5.   Hover cursor over **share with**

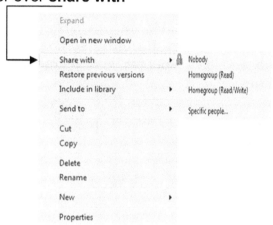

6.   Click who you want to share folder

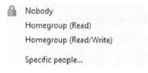

Find Files Faster by Sorting and Filtering

It can be hard to find the file you are looking for in an easy to manage way when you have many of them. By using sorting and filtering, you can narrow down your search and give yourself less to have to look through while also placing them in order.

1.   Click **Start**

2.   Click **Computer**

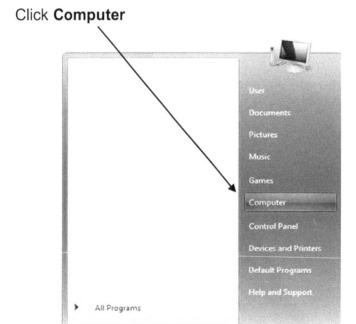

3.   Click **Documents** under **Libraries** or folder location

4.   Click **Folder** next to Arrange by:

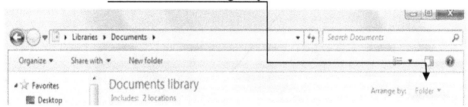

5.   Select sort order

Restore a Previous Version of a File

With the enhanced restore points in *Windows 7*, you do not have to roll back the entire system for small changes. If there is a restore point that contains a previous version of a file, you can restore that particular file to the previous version without any other changes to your system.

1.   Click **Start**

2.   Click **Computer**

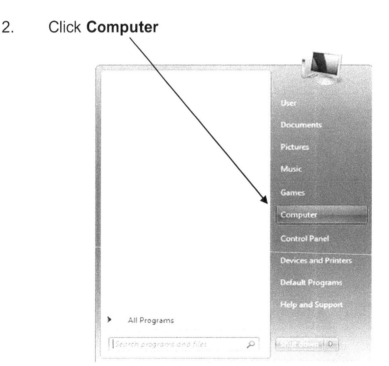

3.　　Click **Documents** under **Libraries** or file location

4.　　Right click file to revert to previous version

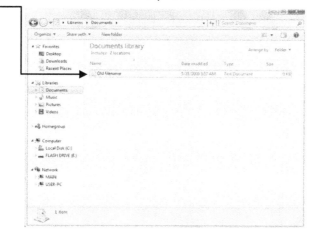

5.   Click **Restore previous versions**

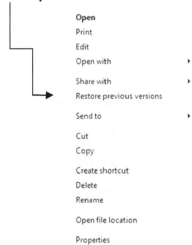

6.   If any previous versions are available, follow instruction. Then click **OK**

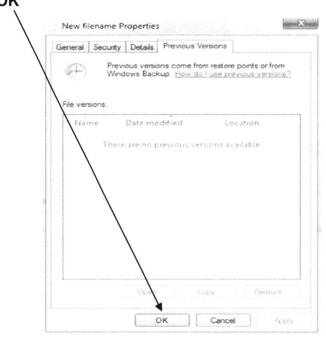

Protect a File by Making It Read-Only

You can protect files from being changed or deleted by mistake by marking them as read only. This will prompt an additional step when trying to delete the file and will prevent it from being changed as well.

1.   Click **Start**

2.   Click **Computer**

3. Click location of file to make read only (example: **Documents** under **Libraries**)

4. Right click file then click **Properties**

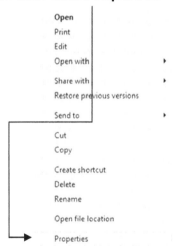

5.   Click **Read only** box then **OK**

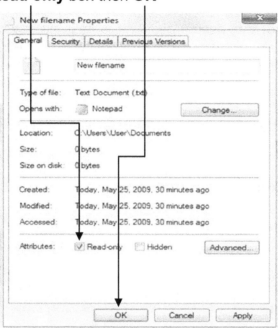

Open a File with a Different Program

The default program associated with a file is not always the one you want to use. If another program would be a better fit for opening your file, you can specify what program you want to use when opening that file.

1.   Click **Start**

2.   Click **Computer**

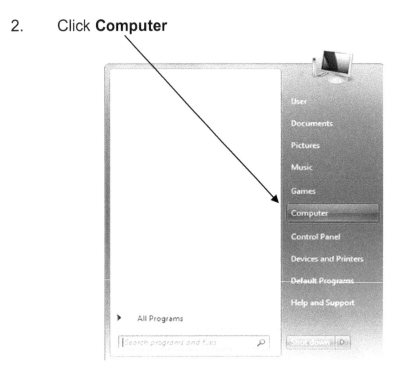

3. Click **Documents** under **Libraries** or file location

4. Click file to open

5. Click ▼ next to **Open**

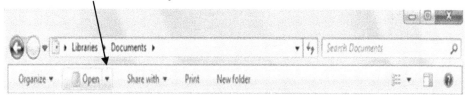

6.   Choose from pull down list or choose Default Program. This will change depending on type of file and programs installed

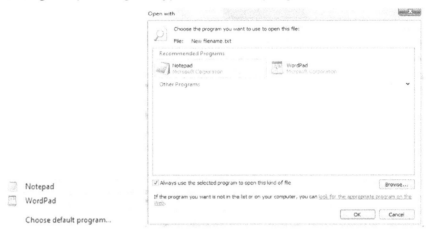

Notepad

WordPad

Choose default program...

Open file or folder with single click

You can set *Windows* to be able to open a file or folder by just clicking on it once, rather than the normal double clicking. This can be useful for people that have a hard time with their hands such as people with arthritis or other ailments that would normally make using a computer difficult.

1.   Click **Start**

2.   Click **Computer**

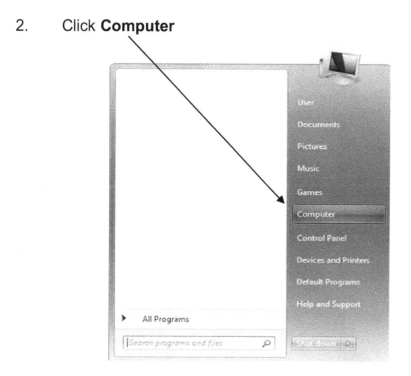

3.   Press **ALT** key

4.   Click **Tools**

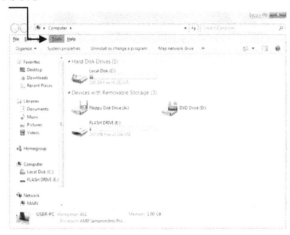

5.   Click **Folder Options** from pull down menu

Map network drive...

Disconnect network drive...

Open Sync Center...

Folder options...

6.   Click so bubble is filled next to **Single-click to open an item (point to select)**, then click **OK**

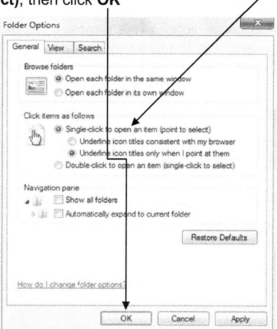

Share drives with other computers

Being able to share the data on your computer with others on your network can be a great convenience. This removes the need to use removable media and physically carry it to the other system back and forth. By sharing the drive, you can access the same data between other computers and have it updated immediately. This can still be done with only a little extra work, which is explained here.

1.   Click **Start**

2.   Click **Computer**

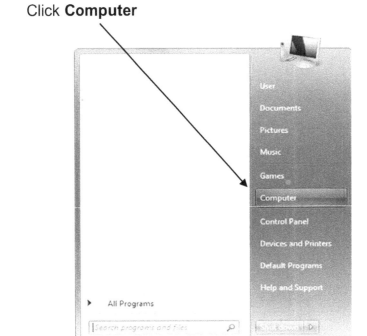

3. Right click on drive to share

4. Click **Properties**

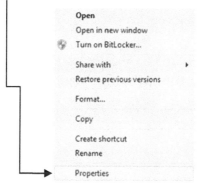

5.   On the **Sharing** tab click **Advanced Sharing…**

6.   Make sure **Share this folder** is marked.

7.   Click **Permissions**

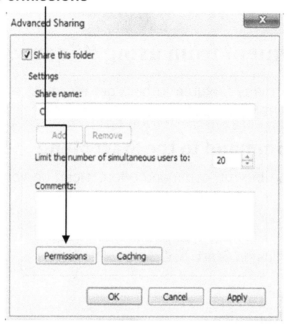

8.   Under **Full Control**, select **Allow** then click **OK**

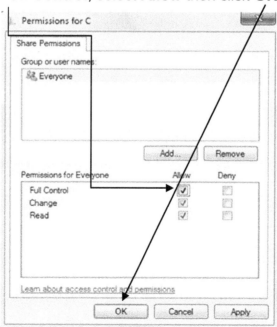

Chapter 7
Getting enjoyment from using *Windows*

Windows has many features to help get the most enjoyment as possible from convenience to music.

Add the Run Command to the Start Menu

If you need to use the run command often, it can be very handy to have this on your start menu.

1.   Right click on **Start**

2.   Click **Properties**

3.　　On the **Start Menu** tab, click **Customize…**

4.　　Select **Run Command**

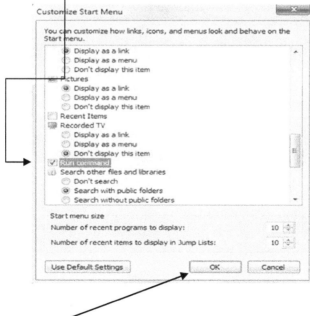

5.　　Click **OK**

Improve Performance with a USB flash Drive (Uses USB as additional system memory)

You can use a USB flash drive to give your computer a performance boost by taking advantage of the ReadyBoost feature. This is a low cost and easy way to get more performance from your computer. Remember the larger and faster the flash drives, the better the performance gain.

1.   Insert USB Flash Drive in port

2.   Click **Speed up my system**

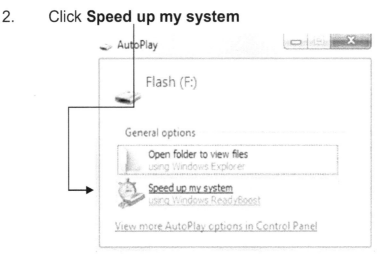

3. Click bubble next to **Dedicate this device to ReadyBoost,** then **OK**

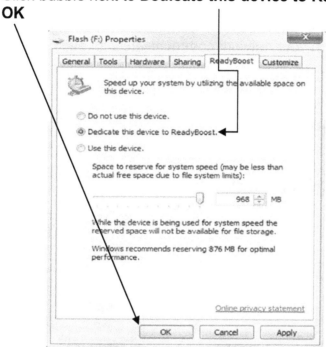

HomeGroup

Homegroup is a new feature in *Windows 7* for making it easy to configure how the computers on your network communicate with each other and how files are shared.

1. Click **Start**

2. Click **Control Panel**

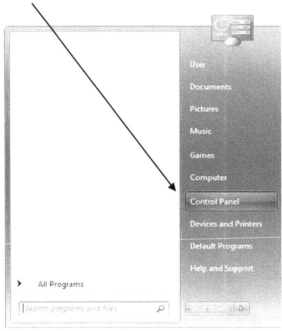

3.   Click **Network and Internet**

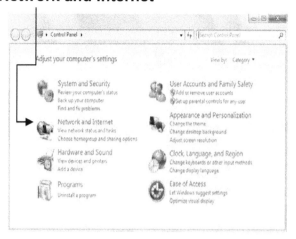

4.   Click **HomeGroup**

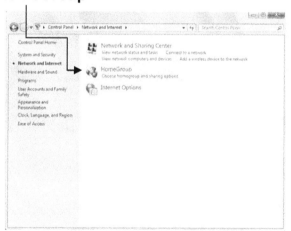

5.   Configure actions according to screen options

Better device management

You do not have to look all over for managing your devices. They can all be found in one location to make it easy to see what *Windows* recognized and be able to adjust them, depending of the device itself.

1.   Click **Start**

2.   Click **Devices and Printers**

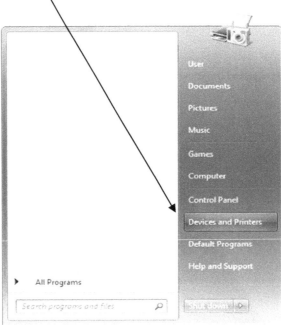

3.   All devices and printers show on one screen instead of several

4.   What can be done depends on selected device. Select a device and the top menu changes. Default printer can be selected.

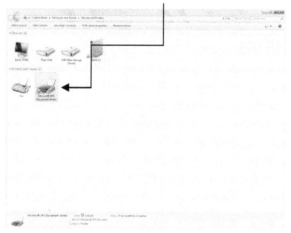

Adjust Rip Settings

If you want to make your own CD, you will need to get the songs on your drive first. You can do this by downloading the songs over the Internet or, if you own CDs with the songs on them, you can copy them to your hard drive in a process known as "ripping"

1.　　Click **Windows Media Player** on Taskbar

2.　　Click **Organize**

3.　　Click **Options...**

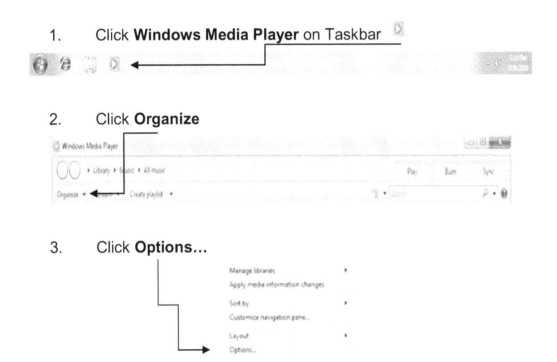

4. Click **Rip Music** tab. Customize preferences and click **OK**

Create an Automatic Playlist

You can set up songs to play in any order you wish and use your computer as a digital music player. This order can be changed or you can make multiple lists without having to use a different CD for each mix.

1.   Click **Windows Media Player** on Taskbar

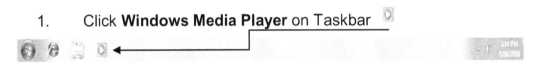

2.   Click **Create Playlist**

3. Enter **playlist name** and press the **ENTER** key

4. Click the name of playlist just created and follow instructions in center window

Chapter 8
Presenting with *Windows*

Windows had several functions built in for using it for graphics and text documents as well as interacting with others with built in Fax capability.

Rotate an Image

When you get a picture, by downloading or from a camera or scanner, it might not be oriented with the top being up. The picture can be easily changed to have it right side up for easier viewing.

1.   Click **Start**

2.   Click **All Programs**

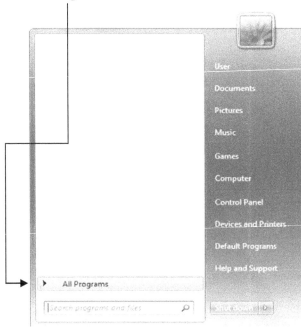

3.   Click **Accessories**

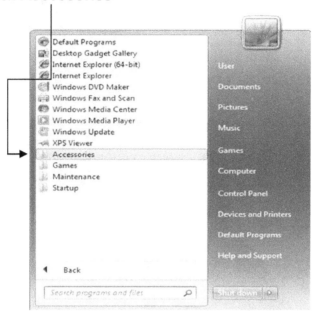

4.   Click **Paint**

5. Click to reveal pull down menu

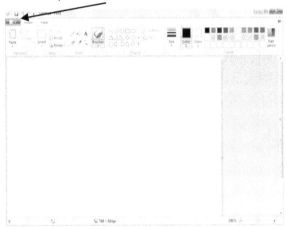

6. Click **Open**

7.   Open picture to be rotated

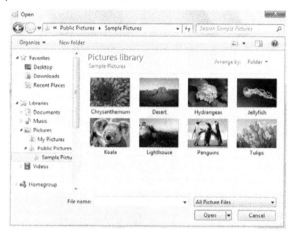

6.   Click **Rotate** for pull down menu

7.   Click direction to rotate picture

Rotate right 90°

Rotate left 90°

Rotate 180°

Flip vertical

Flip horizontal

Snipping Tool

Taking screen captures has become much easier in *Windows 7* with the Snipping Tool. This allows you to take a screen capture of nearly anything on your screen and save it to a file by just dragging a selection marker around what you want and giving it a filename.

1.   Click **Start**

2.   Click **All Programs**

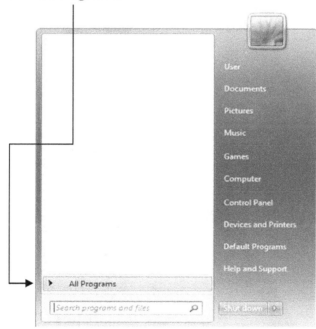

3. Click **Accessories**

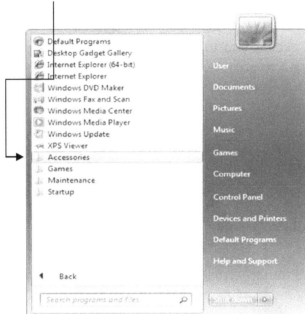

4. Click **Snipping Tool**

8.   Select capture type from the pull down menu by clicking ▼

9.   Select area to capture

10.   Once image is captured, select what should be done with it

Basics of *Windows 7*

Fax and Scan

Windows has built-in software to handle faxing and scanning. From here, you can send and receive faxes, scan pictures and documents, and even send anything from here to an email address.

1.   Click **Start**

2.   Click **All Programs**

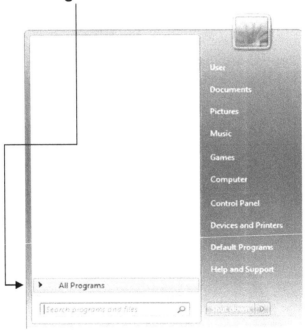

3.   Click **Windows Fax and Scan**

4.   Click on appropriate button or review instructions on screen

Basics of *Windows 7*

Magnifier

For those with less than perfect eyesight, reading the screen can be a challenge. To help compensate for this, *Windows* has an on-screen magnifier to enlarge the area of the screen which you are trying to read. This enlargement can be adjusted to best suit your need and position on the screen.

1. Click **Start**

2. Click **All Programs**

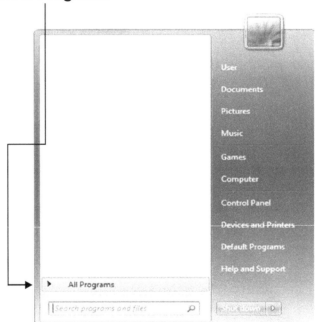

3.   Click **Accessories**

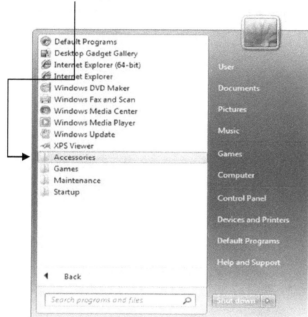

4.   Click **Ease of Access**

5.   Click **Magnifier**

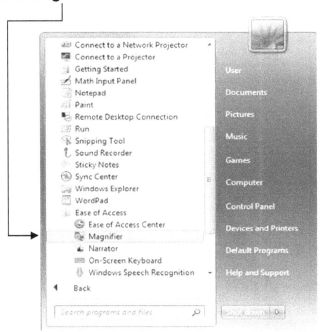

6.   Click the gear icon for options.

NOTE: when cursor is not on this box for three seconds or it is not the

active window it will be replaced by   . To show box move cursor to

icon   then click »

7.   Select how magnifier should behave then click **OK**

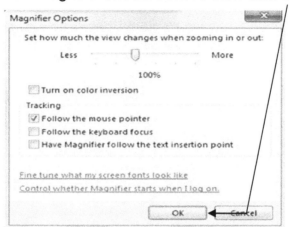

Speech Recognition

Before, sci-fi shows always depicted being able to talk to your computer and the words showing up on the screen. With speech recognition in *Windows 7* you can control your computer, as well as dictate to it and have the words appear on the screen for you without typing.

1.   Click **Start**

2.   Click **All Programs**

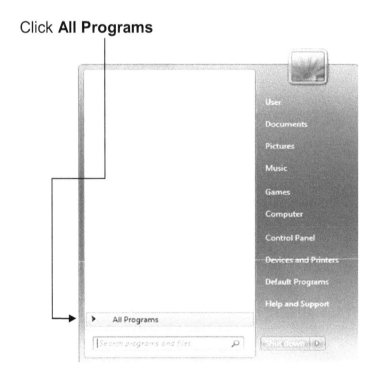

3.   Click **Accessories**

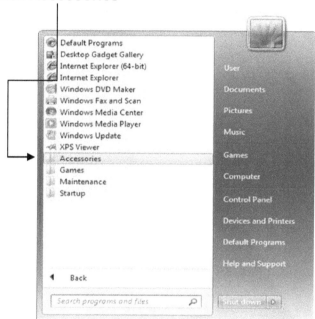

4.   Click **Ease of Access**

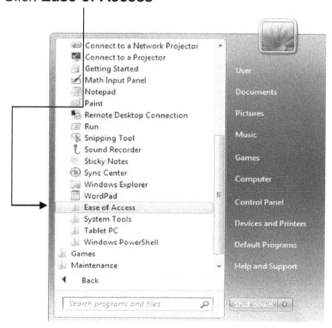

5.   Click **Windows Speech Recognition**

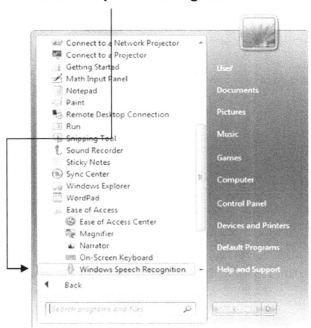

6.   Read screen before clicking **Next**

7.   Select what best describes the device used and then click **Next**

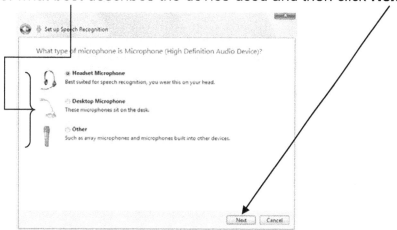

8.   Read screen before clicking **Next**

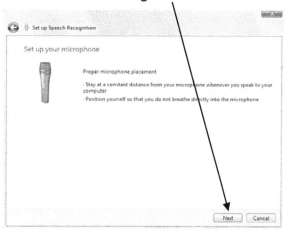

9.   Follow the instructions on the screen and then click **Next**

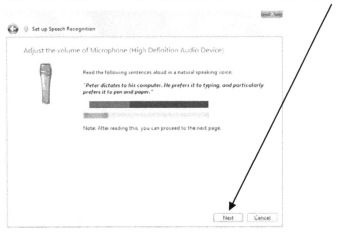

10.   Read screen before clicking **Next**

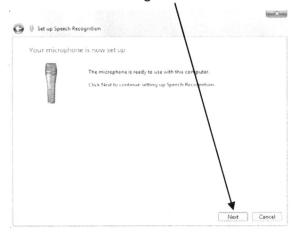

11. Select choice after reading the screen and then click **Next**

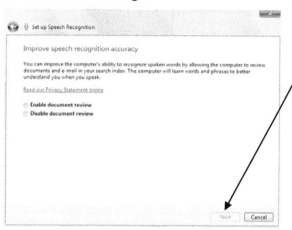

12. Select choice after reading the screen and then click **Next**

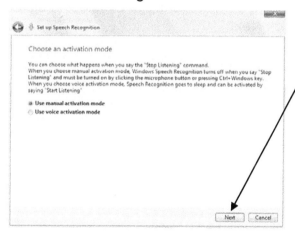

13. Click **View Reference Sheet** to see or print the list of commands and then click **Next**

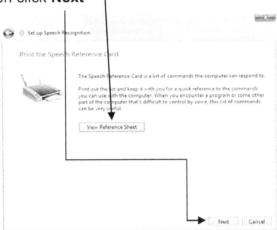

14. Default is to start at startup or unselect to disable this option and then click **Next**

15.   Highly recommend using the **tutorial** until comfortable with this option.

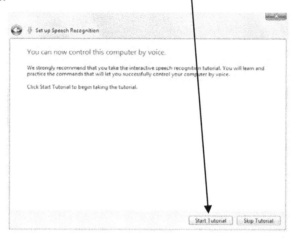

Manually start Speech Recognition

1.   Click **Start**

2.   Click **All Programs**

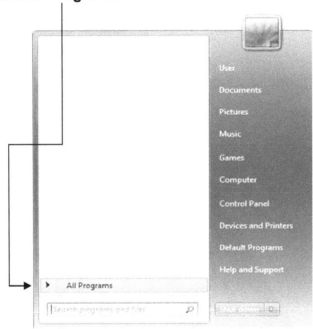

3.   Click **Accessories**

4.   Click **Ease of Access**

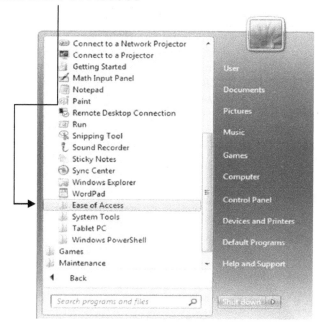

5. Click **Windows Speech Recognition**

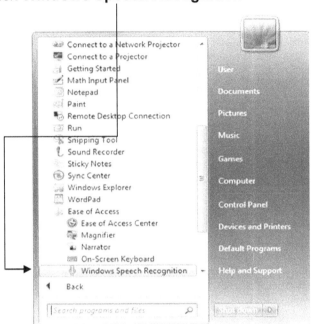

6. Toggle can turn on/off Speech Recognition

7. Right click on bar for options

8. Make selection or exit

Notepad or WordPad

Windows comes with two programs to allow you to do text or document editing and creation. For doing basic text jobs, Notepad is the best bet, as it is very basic, making it simple to use. If you need something more advanced so you can change text size, fonts, colors, etc. then WordPad would be the program of choice.

1.   Click **Start**

2.   Click **All Programs**

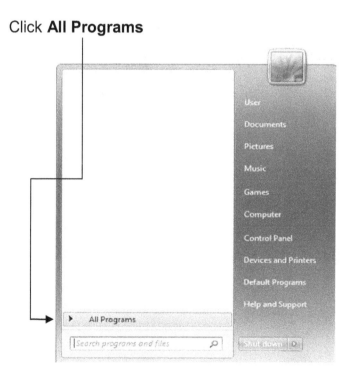

3.   Click **Accessories**

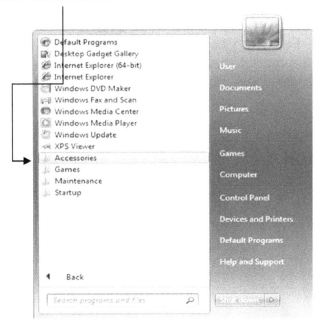

Notepad

1.   For plain text, click **Notepad**

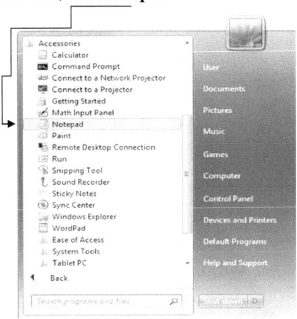

2.   Type for plain text editing

OR

WordPad

1. For basic word processing, click **WordPad**

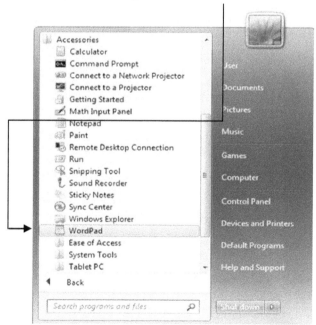

2.   Offers many options for entering text (i.e. font size, color, formatting, etc)

Windows Live Essentials

Microsoft has grouped all of their additional features into a downloadable bundle called *Windows Live Essentials*. This provides the user with instant messaging, email client software, and many other optional functions.

1. Download via Windows Update or direct from *Windows Live Essentials* site (Download.Live.com)

2. Click on **program** name for a brief **description**. **Uncheck** program(s) not wanted and **check** program(s) wanted then click **install**

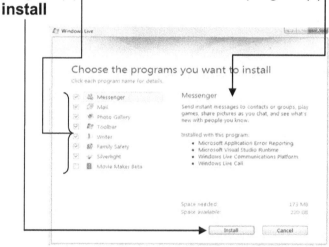

3.   Go take a break while waiting for installation to complete.

4.   Select you setting preferences and click **Continue**

5.   Read screen, sign up for the ***Windows Live ID*** or click **Close**

Terms

Background

The image behind the Icons on the desktop. It can be a color, pattern or picture.

Click

A quick press and release of the left mouse button without moving the mouse.

Collapse

Reduce size so options are no longer displayed.

Commonly used control buttons

Located on upper right corner of most windows

Click ⊠ in the upper-right corner to close a window,

Click ⬜ to minimize the window to a taskbar button. To restore the minimized window to its previous size, click its taskbar button

Click ⬜ to maximize the window so it covers the full screen

Click ⬜ to restore the window to its previous size after maximizing.

Defragment

Reorganizes data so it can be accessed more efficiently.

Desktop

The main section of the *Windows* interface when no programs are open.

Double click

Two quick presses and releases of the left mouse button in rapid succession without moving the mouse

Drag

Holding down a mouse button, usually the left button, and moving the mouse at the same time to a new location prior to releasing the button.

Expand

To increase in size for displaying additional options

Hover

To position the mouse pointer over a location and leave it there.

Icon

A picture used to represent a program, file, or action.

Malware

A general term for all kinds of malicious software intended to cause harm to a computer or otherwise perform undesired functions.

Pull down menu

A menu that once you select it will display additional options.

Right click

A quick press and release of the right mouse button without moving the mouse.

Scroll/scroll bar

Scroll- To move a display within a window that cannot display everything at once.

Scroll bar-The indicator at the since or bottom showing where the current view is In reference to the entire display

Select

To choice an object so that you can manipulate it in some way

Spyware

A type of malware that record and reports to others what is on your computer. Often causes the computer to run slow and/or crash similar to a virus.

Taskbar

Display, usually at the bottom of the desktop that contains the Start menu, Clock, and all the active and quick launch program icons.

Theme

A general scheme of how a *Windows* user environment appears.

Thumbnail

A small version of a picture.

Virus

A type of malware that is designed to cause harm to a computer. Often designed to protect itself, spread to other computers, and sometime remain dormant for an amount of time before activating.

Index

A

accounts 121, 124, 127, 128

add user *see* accounts

alphabetical order *see* sorting

appearance 9, 14

B

background 1, 4, 9, 13, 14, 22, 223

backup 44, 45, 47

C

click 223

collapse 223

commonly used control buttons 223

compatibility mode 42, 43

control panel 36, 85, 86, 89, 94, 99, 102, 106, 109, 113, 117, 120, 123, 127, 130, 133, 137, 141, 145, 184

D

default 1, 4, 9, 27, 54, 102, 115, 136, 137, 151, 170, 172, 187, 212

defragment 150, 152, 223

delete user *see* accounts

desktop 1, 4, 6, 9, 11, 12, 13, 14, 21, 40, 54, 223

disk defragmenter *see* defragment

double click 40, 54, 104, 137, 140, 173, 224

double click speed 137, 140

drag 3, 18, 19, 40, 93, 140, 197, 224

drive letter 102, 105, 156, 158

E

energy savings *see* power plan

expand 29, 224

F

fax and scan 200, 201

file sharing *see* sharing

filename 149, 150, 197

flash drive 182

H

hard drive 44, 48, 143, 188

hover 6, 7, 9, 161, 224

I

icon 3, 9, 11, 12, 20, 22, 40, 61, 63, 66, 68, 71, 73, 75, 78, 80, 81, 83, 142, 146, 204, 224

internet explorer 20, 61, 63, 66, 68, 71, 73, 75, 76, 77, 78, 79, 80, 81, 83

internet options 63, 66, 68, 75

M

magnifier 202, 204, 205

media player *see* Windows Media Player

music 113, 145, 180, 189, 190

N

network 106, 107, 109, 110, 113, 114, 156, 158, 159, 176, 184, 185

P

parental controls 63, 64

password 25, 120, 121, 122, 123, 124, 125, 126

power options 95, 100

power plan 94, 96
properties 21, 27, 39, 43, 136, 154, 168, 177, 180

pull down menu 2, 15, 16, 17, 22, 24, 28, 43, 53, 97, 101, 116, 142, 146, 158, 174, 194, 195, 199, 224

R

ReadyBoost 182, 183

recycle bin 54, 55, 56

remove programs 36

renaming 148, 150, 151, 152

resolution 1, 2, 3, 4

restart 28

restore point 57, 60, 164

right click 224

run command 180, 181

S

scanner 192

scroll 98, 130, 225

scroll bar 225

select 5, 10, 12, 14, 15, 16, 21, 23, 24, 28, 29, 43, 50, 70, 78, 88, 92, 97, 101, 119, 132, 135, 136, 139, 147, 155, 158, 163, 175, 179, 181, 187, 199, 205, 209, 211, 212, 222, 225

sharing 107, 110, 113, 114, 115, 116, 159, 176, 178

sharing files and folders *see* sharing

shut down 25, 27, 28

snipping tool 197, 198

sorting 162

speech recognition 206, 208, 214, 216

spyware 141, 225

start menu 32, 33, 34, 35, 180, 181

system restore 57, 59

T

taskbar 9, 20, 21, 23, 29, 31, 32, 34, 35, 61, 63, 66, 68, 71, 73, 75, 78, 80, 81, 83, 188, 190, 225

theme 1, 9, 10, 13, 225

thumbnail 6, 9, 10, 72, 225

U

uninstall a program 36, 37

W

Windows Defender 141, 142

Windows Fax and Scan *see* Fax and Scan

Windows Media Player 188, 190

Windows Update 48, 49, 221

Windows Media Player 188, 190

Windows Update 48, 49, 221